WASHINGTON DC

THE CITY AT A GL

GH01044293

National Building Muse
The great hall of Montgo
landmark has immense (
401 F Street NW, T 202 2

Verizon Center
A block of Chinatown devoted to ice hockey
and hoops, the 1997 Verizon Center helped
revive this once flagging part of Downtown.
601 F Street NW, T 202 661 5000

Capitol
An architectural and political bookend to
the Mall, the dome of this structure is iron,
but painted to look like a marble beacon.
1st Street/E Capitol Street, T 202 226 8000

National Gallery of Art
In 1978, IM Pei designed a modernist east
wing for this neoclassical 1941 building.
See p070

Hirshhorn Museum
Gordon Bunshaft's concrete drum stands out
amid the Mall's wedding-cake architecture.
See p065

White House
One of the world's best-known landmarks
is unfortunately strangled by security.
See p010

Washington Monument
Directly in line with the Capitol and Lincoln
Memorial (see p014), this iconic monument
punctuates L'Enfant's *grande allée*.
National Mall

Thomas Jefferson Memorial
Spot the typos (chiselos) in the Declaration
of Independence here in leafy Elysium.
701 E Basin Drive, T 202 426 6841

INTRODUCTION
THE CHANGING FACE OF THE URBAN SCENE

In the 1990s, Washington DC had an image problem. The capital may have been full of tourists and politicos, but it was also racially divided, its wealthy white minority corralled into the north-west quarter. It had a reputation as America's murder capital; the mayor, Marion Barry, was charged with possession of cocaine in 1990; and whole streets near the centre had never recovered from the riots after the assassination of Martin Luther King Jr. Cut to today, nearly 25 years later, and one can see a marked cultural evolution.

The Ethiopian eateries and El Salvadorian bars in hip, mixed Adams Morgan always defied the divisive trend, and from here a new kind of town has grown – spreading east along the old 'Black Broadway' of U Street, a predominantly African-American district that now boasts new restaurants and clubs, and enveloping parts of 14th Street that were once no-go areas. The always transitory, politically addicted denizens of DC have discovered the delights of inner-city living again. Even the shabby stretch of H Street, east of Union Station, has started to see not just gentrification but local entrepreneurs bringing a new lease of life into their communities.

And in the monument-heavy middle, excellent museums, such as the one dedicated to Native Americans (see p068), tell the story of the whole nation, matching the egalitarian sentiments inscribed in so much of the marble here, in what Charles Dickens called the 'city of magnificent intentions'. Go see for yourself.

ESSENTIAL INFO

FACTS, FIGURES AND USEFUL ADDRESSES

TOURIST OFFICE
Destination DC
901 7th Street
T 202 789 7000
www.washington.org

TRANSPORT
Airport transfer to city centre
An express bus service operates to and
from L'Enfant Plaza, which connects to the
metro. The journey takes 40 to 50 minutes
www.metwashairports.com/dulles
Car hire
Enterprise
1029 Vermont Avenue
T 202 393 0900
Metro
Trains run from 5am, Mon to Fri, and from
7am at the weekend; until 3am, Fri to Sat,
and 12am, Sun to Thurs. A SmarTrip card
can be used on Metrorail and Metrobus
T 202 962 1234
www.wmata.com
Taxis
Diamond Cab
T 202 387 6200
Cabs can be hailed in the street, but they
do not accept payment by credit card

EMERGENCY SERVICES
Emergencies
T 911
24-hour pharmacy
CVS Pharmacy
6 Dupont Circle NW
T 202 785 1466

EMBASSY
British Embassy
3100 Massachusetts Avenue NW
T 202 588 6500
www.gov.uk/government/world/usa

POSTAL SERVICES
Post Office
416 Florida Avenue NW
T 202 483 0973
Shipping
FedEx
1029 17th Street NW
T 202 659 2833

BOOKS
All the President's Men by Carl Bernstein
and Bob Woodward (Simon & Schuster)
**The Hidden White House: Harry
Truman and the Reconstruction of
America's Most Famous Residence** by
Robert Klara (Thomas Dunne Books)

WEBSITES
Architecture
www.nbm.org
Newspapers
www.washingtoncitypaper.com
www.washingtonpost.com

EVENTS
DC Design Week
www.dc.aiga.org
Emerge Art Fair
www.emergeartfair.com

COST OF LIVING
**Taxi from Dulles International
Airport to city centre**
$68
Cappuccino
$2.70
Packet of cigarettes
$8
Daily newspaper
$1
Bottle of champagne
$40

WASHINGTON DC
Population
632,000
Currency
US dollar
Telephone codes
USA: 1
Washington DC: 202
Local time
GMT -5
Flight time
London: 7 hrs 50 mins

Montreal
Toronto
Boston
New York
Philadelphia
Chicago
Washington DC

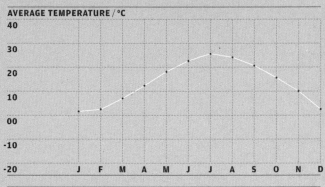

AVERAGE TEMPERATURE / °C

40												
30												
20												
10												
00												
-10												
-20	J	F	M	A	M	J	J	A	S	O	N	D

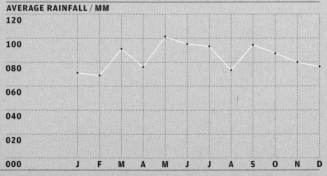

AVERAGE RAINFALL / MM

120												
100												
080												
060												
040												
020												
000	J	F	M	A	M	J	J	A	S	O	N	D

NEIGHBOURHOODS

THE AREAS YOU NEED TO KNOW AND WHY

To help you navigate the city, we've chosen the most interesting districts (see below and the map inside the back cover) and colour-coded our featured venues, according to their location; those venues that are outside these areas are not coloured.

GEORGETOWN

This pretty suburb overlooks the Potomac River and heaves with tourists, students and preppie Republicans at the weekend. Stay at the Capella (see p020) and shop, sup or duck off the bar-crowded M Street to wander the tree-lined avenues of red-brick, Federal-style millionaires' homes.

ADAMS MORGAN

Named after the merging of an African-American and a white school in 1955, Adams Morgan led the way in integration. Now 18th Street jumps with restaurants, bars and hangouts of every hue and creed. Weekends can become so bridge-and-tunnel, police close the main drag to cars.

NATIONAL MALL

Probably the greatest collection of globally famous landmarks anywhere on the planet. Pick your targets carefully – the Capitol (see p009), the White House (see p010), the Lincoln Memorial (see p014), to name just a few – or you might join the tourist throng who never see the rest of the city.

U STREET/14TH STREET CORRIDOR

Much of U Street was burnt out in the riots of 1968 and then abandoned to drug dealers and gangs for almost three decades. Out of the ashes has grown a zone of hip bars, restaurants and clubs, such as Café Saint-Ex (see p056), and interesting local stores like GoodWood (see p062) and Redeem (see p080).

FOGGY BOTTOM

The west end of Downtown is the place to see what rare modernist beauties the city boasts – the Kennedy Center (2700 F Street NW, T 202 467 4600), Watergate Complex (see p012) and the Pan-American Health Organisation HQ (see p072). It's also home to several upscale hotels.

DOWNTOWN

Come here to see Mies van der Rohe's library building (see p074) and some delightful galleries and museums, such as the National Portrait Gallery (see p036), in the Penn Quarter. Pose among the beautiful people at sophisticated haunts like the cocktail bar Barmini (see p038).

DUPONT CIRCLE

Embassies cluster here, gay bookshops proliferate and the counterculture once gathered around this traffic circle. Now, despite a big-business takeover, you'll find an upmarket bar scene, eateries such as Hank's Oyster Bar (see p045), and cafés and dive bars to the north and the east.

CAPITOL HILL

Not that long ago, there were slums five minutes from Congress. Now the area east of the Capitol is packed with politicians (although none quite as attractive as the folk in *Scandal*) who scheme and plot in the bars of Pennsylvania Avenue and the pet-grooming parlours around the chichi Eastern Market neighbourhood.

LANDMARKS

THE SHAPE OF THE CITY SKYLINE

French engineer Pierre Charles L'Enfant's planned capital district, with its grand avenues and awe-inspiring heart, was an exercise in hubris when it was laid out in the 1790s. America was 13 barely united colonies, and Washington was a swampy frontier town that saw in the 19th century with a White House (overleaf), Capitol building (1st Street/E Capitol Street, T 202 226 8000) and not much else. But the genius of the Frenchman's plan was that it left space to insert the imperious buildings, museums and war memorials that the superpower would generate over the next 200-odd years.

You are, quite frankly, spoilt for choice with the abundance of internationally recognisable landmarks here. Making your way along Pennsylvania Avenue and up the National Mall, stopping off at everything along the way, would leave you no time for the rest of the city. However, there are sights that are unmissable, either for their political resonance, such as the Lincoln Memorial (see p014) and the Vietnam Veterans Memorial (Constitution Gardens, T 202 426 6841), or for their blend of controversy and modernism, such as the Watergate Complex (see p012). They're all linked by the municipal triumph that is the Washington Metro. Designed mostly by the Chicago-based architect Harry Weese and opened in 1976, the capital's subway system is a pioneering example of how architecture and engineering can combine in perfect harmony. *For full addresses, see Resources.*

White House

This is most definitely not the presidential palace, not in this republic. People followed Thomas Jefferson here after his inauguration in 1801 and had a party, and in 1829 Andrew Jackson fled to a hotel after his, while 20,000 people got tanked on whisky in his 'mud-tracked house'. Built between 1792 and 1800, this neoclassical Georgian pile was designed by James Hoban, an Irishman from South Carolina, with Yorkshireman Benjamin Latrobe conceiving the distinctive north and south colonnaded porticoes, added after the British burned the building down in 1814. Some claim the north elevation is a copy of Leinster House in Dublin. The view from the south (left) is the most familiar, and the Oval Office is on the first floor of the West Wing if you feel like waving. Tours can be arranged through your embassy or congressman.
1600 Pennsylvania Avenue, T 202 456 7041

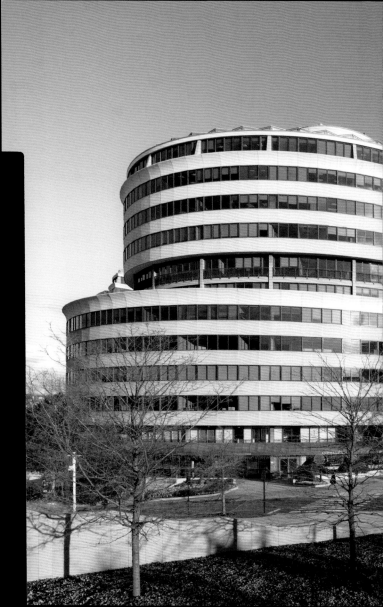

Watergate Complex

Built between 1964 and 1971, these six massive buildings, designed by Italian architect Luigi Moretti in a modernist style, remain desirable real estate.
In June 1972, five men working for the Committee to Re-elect the President (Nixon) were arrested breaking into the Democratic Party offices here. Now any political scandal adopts the '-gate' suffix.
2600 Virginia Avenue

Lincoln Memorial
Modelled on a Greek Doric temple, Henry Bacon's 1922 memorial is the place to rally while calling down Lincoln's moral authority to your cause. The destination of the March on Washington for Jobs and Freedom on 28 August 1963, this is where Martin Luther King Jr had his dream. Inside is sculptor Daniel Chester French's legendary seated Lincoln.
Constitution Gardens, T 202 426 6841

HOTELS

WHERE TO STAY AND WHICH ROOMS TO BOOK

Some of DC's venerable hotels are practically national monuments themselves. Several boast key roles in American history, usually of the less salubrious kind, such as ushering in the era of lobbyists or functioning as the hiding place of the presidential mistress. The high rollers of industry and international affairs who come calling on power keep up the demand for five-star pampering, but the sheer number of rooms at the luxury end means the local market stays competitive. Most of the historic hotels, such as The Jefferson (see p018), have undergone relatively recent multimillion-dollar makeovers, and all of them are spruced up for the four-yearly, full-occupancy beanfeast that is a presidential inauguration.

But you only have to look at how politicians dress to know most DC hotels are far from cutting-edge. Although the service is great, you get an excess of gilt and heavy-duty swagging. Fortunately, more design-savvy hotel groups have a presence too, and there are modish places to rest your head, like Kimpton's Hotel Monaco (see p024) and Donovan House (see p030), the Park Hyatt (see p028), and the much anticipated Capella (see p020), which has opened in Georgetown. The fierce rivalry has also spread to DC's hotel kitchens, and the weapon they all use in the fight to stay on top is an in-house celebrity chef. Thankfully, you do not have to make a three-months-in-advance reservation for room service. *For full addresses and room rates, see Resources.*

The Willard InterContinental

History stalks the corridors of The Willard, situated just two blocks from the White House (see p010). Lincoln stayed here the night before his inauguration in 1861, and Grant used to come in every evening for a drink (special interest groups waited to collar him in the lobby, hence the term 'lobbyists'). This is also the place where Martin Luther King Jr finished writing his 'I have a dream' speech. Although it is hardly a design destination – the lobby (above) is a riot of pillars and potted palms – a renovation in 2000 means it now has modern amenities as well as four-posters. If you're feeling romantic, stay in the Jenny Lind Suite, a garret featuring a wrought-iron bed and a sunken jacuzzi overlooking the Washington Monument. *1401 Pennsylvania Avenue NW, T 202 628 9100, www.washington.intercontinental.com*

The Jefferson
Originally an apartment block built in the 1920s, designed by Jules Henri de Sibour, this elegant Beaux Arts building was turned into a hotel in the 1950s. In 2009, it emerged from a revamp (lobby, pictured), during which time a domed skylight that had been covered over in WWII was revealed. Reserve a Deluxe Room and eat at the acclaimed Plume.
1200 16th Street NW, T 202 448 2300

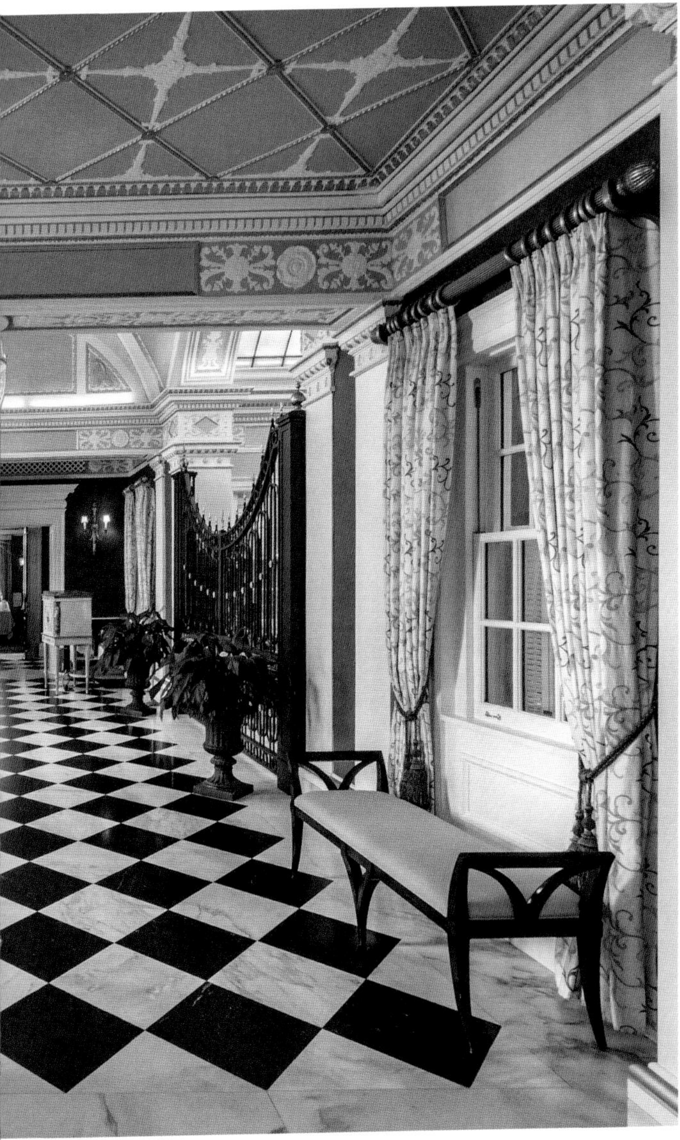

Capella

Unveiled in 2013, this new DC arrival, the Capella brand's first American property, has styled itself as a slick urban retreat, with an explicit emphasis on service – an abundance of concierge benefits are on offer round the clock. The hotel sits on the C&O Canal, a 19th-century trade route linking the Potomac and the Ohio River in Pennsylvania – a location that puts guests at the heart of tony Georgetown. Designer Peter Silling gave the 49 rooms and suites, such as the Georgetown Room (above), a decor that nods to the historic locale but keeps the feel contemporary. The indoor rooftop infinity pool (opposite) is useable throughout the year and is a real success, with superb views. Dine in The Grill Room, on chef Jakob Esko's modern American cuisine, or settle into the clubby Rye Bar, which has a pleasant outdoor terrace.
1050 31st Street NW, T 202 617 2400,
www.capellahotels.com/washingtondc

Hotel Tabard Inn

Providing a characterful alternative to DC's marble-and-history-heavy palaces, the Tabard Inn is a non-corporate island of shabby chic, popular with journalists, academic types and those who don't mind the lack of an elevator. It's made up of three adjoining 19th-century townhouses, and has been owned by the Cohen family since the 1970s. Interior designer Irene Mayer was hired to do the decorating, and she ensured that no two rooms look alike. The hotel has one of the cosiest bars in town, which fills up with an eclectic crowd ranging from hipsters to sober lobbyists, and a surprisingly upscale restaurant, now overseen by chef Paul Pelt. Room 42 (above and opposite) has an attractive iron bedstead and a bright adjoining bathroom. *1739 N Street NW, T 202 785 1277, www.tabardinn.com*

Hotel Monaco

Part of the Kimpton group, the Monaco is
an example of what good design can do
for a heritage building. Largely the work
of Robert Mills, who was the architect of
the Washington Monument, this Penn
Quarter building was completed in 1839
and has since housed various government
entities, including the city's very first post
office and the Tariff Office. After several
years lying vacant, it was transformed into
this classy hotel by LA-based designer
Cheryl Rowley in 2002. The decor, as in the
lobby (right), is eclectic, with a nice blend
of classic and contemporary furnishings,
pattern and punchy colours. Oversized
lighting counterbalances the large ceilings.
Opt for Room 316, which looks on to the
chef's garden in the inner courtyard.
700 F Street NW, T 202 628 7177,
www.monaco-dc.com

The Mayflower Renaissance

The dowager duchess of DC hotels, the 1925 Mayflower is as integral to American politics as a Kennedy or a Bush. Truman stayed here for the first three months of his term; Roosevelt lived here before his inauguration and dictated his 'The only thing we have to fear is fear itself' speech in Room 776; and JFK's alleged mistress used to wait here for Jackie to go out. More recently, this is where Hillary Clinton introduced Barack Obama to her key contributors in 2008. It'll never be a hip hangout, but renovation has uncovered much of the gilt and an impressive skylight that add to the splendour of the lobby (above). The rooms are sumptuous and muscular in their decor, as befits a hotel where power oozes from the furnishings.
1127 Connecticut Avenue NW,
T 202 347 3000, www.marriott.com

Hotel Palomar

The arty Palomar could be seen as one of those hotels that thinks it's an elite club. But despite the chic Dupont Circle address and contemporary interiors, the staff are anything but snooty, doling out free wine in the early evening, and putting a goldfish in your room if you get lonely. The rooms are huge for the price, with a third of the building given over to Executive Kings that have floor-to-ceiling windows.

Designer Cheryl Rowley, who also did the Monaco (see p024), used a range of solid, dark colours with the occasional splash of animal print (the throws on the bed are faux fur, as you'd expect from a hotel that prides itself on being pet-friendly). Book Room 922 (above) or 939, the Spa Suite, which comes with a Fuji soaking tub. *2121 P Street NW, T 202 448 1800, www.hotelpalomardc.com*

Park Hyatt

Designer Tony Chi's $26m reworking of the Park Hyatt in 2006 lifted what was a tired corporate giant into the city's top tier of accommodation. Out went the trad luxury features; in came clean lines and modernist touches combined with pieces by some of America's most talented artisans. There are bespoke light fixtures by David Singer and American Windsor chairs by Vermont furniture-maker Timothy Clark in the lobby. Even the least expensive guest rooms are generously sized, and feature limestone-lined bathrooms with great showers; we suggest going one step up by booking a Park Deluxe, such as Room 916 (above). Conveniently close to Dupont Circle, the hotel also boasts the respected Blue Duck Tavern (T 202 419 6755). *1201 24th Street NW, T 202 789 1234, www.parkwashington.hyatt.com*

Four Seasons

Located on the edge of Georgetown, the Four Seasons has had more than $40m lavished on it since 2005. Regular Four Seasons collaborator Pierre-Yves Rochon oversaw the redesign of the rooms, in grand luxe style, while Pamela Anderson of Midwest firm Anderson/Miller gave the hotel six more up-to-date Presidential Suites in 2008, such as Room 478 in the West Wing (above), and Room 278, which has bulletproof windows. New York-based interior designer David Rockwell created the Bourbon Steak restaurant for founding chef Michael Mina. But more important is the stratospheric level of service. Staff are so inordinately helpful and attentive, it's almost like being stalked – even the gardeners will remember your name.
2800 Pennsylvania Avenue NW, T 202 342 0444, www.fourseasons.com/washington

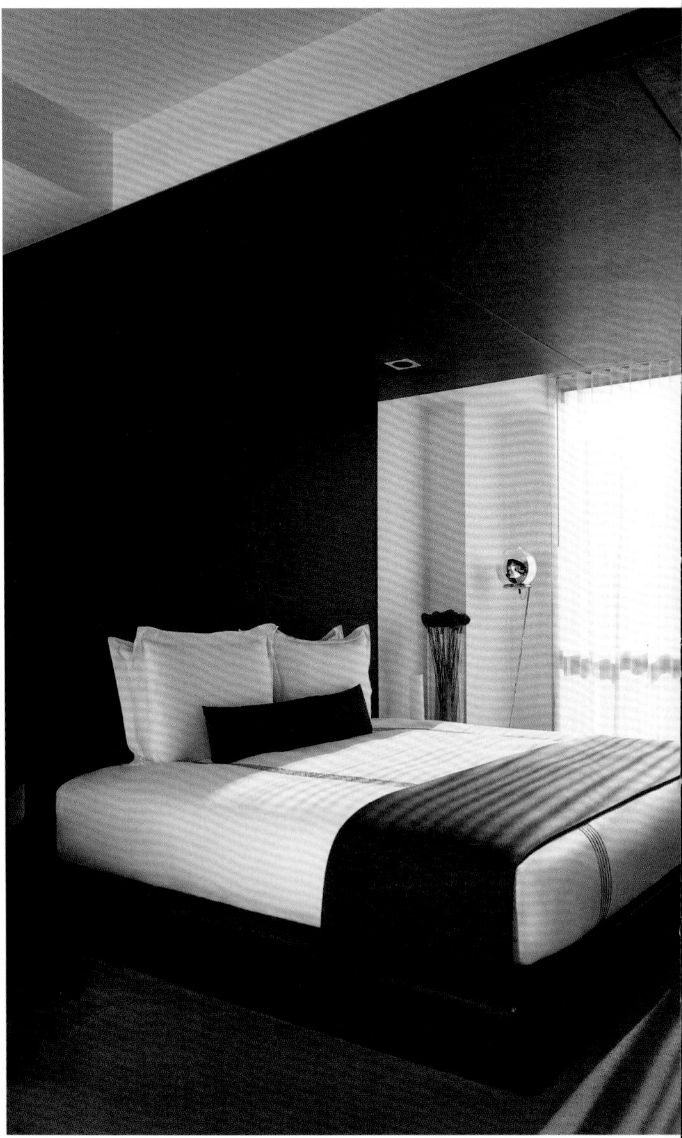

Donovan House

When this boutique hotel launched in Downtown in March 2008, it created a buzz in the local media by advertising for 'good-looking revolutionaries' to staff it. Needless to say, the fashionistas who showed up wouldn't have been seen dead at the Holiday Inn that was here before the multimillion-dollar renovation by Ilan Waisbrod of New York-based Studio Gaia. Taken over by the Kimpton group in 2012, the hotel, named after 'Wild Bill' Donovan, founder of the Office of Strategic Services, which became the CIA, has retained its snazzy feel. We like the Studio King Suites (left). Further renovations were initiated in 2014, updating the interiors, including the lobby and guest rooms. The rooftop was reimagined by the Washington design firm GrizForm, who created a sleek bar called DNV, which has expansive views.
1155 14th Street NW, T 202 737 1200,
www.donovanhousehotel.com

24 HOURS

SEE THE BEST OF THE CITY IN JUST ONE DAY

There's a lot to see in DC. If time is tight, we suggest you make a beeline for the less obvious sights, avoiding the populist picks such as the National Air and Space Museum (Independence Avenue, T 202 633 2214), which is all a bit boys' toys for us. Instead, head to the Atlas District centred on H Street to tour the contemporary art galleries Industry (1358 Florida Avenue NE, T 202 399 1730), which focuses on design, Connorsmith (see p034) and G Fine Art (see p086); call ahead to each venue as opening times can vary. We saved the Hirshhorn Museum (see p065), with its impressive sculpture garden and collection of works by Alberto Giacometti and Willem de Kooning, among many others, for another chapter, opting here for the National Portrait Gallery (see p036), a piece of striking contemporary architecture to showcase art that tells the story of a nation through its most eminent people.

Our dining choices reflect the diversity of DC. Ben's Chili Bowl (see p050), for lunch, may not be the hippest eatery in town but it's one of the most authentic. In contrast, dinner is at Proof (see p037), where the food is modern and sophisticated. We end the day at Barmini (see p038), a new-wave cocktail bar with an innovative edge. Or you could sample the old-school Dixie delights of the Round Robin Bar at the Willard (see p017), a place that challenges JFK's remark that DC is all Southern efficiency and Northern charm. *For full addresses, see Resources.*

10.00 Batter Bowl Bakery

Samuel Ergete and Meseret Bekele's first venture in the Atlas District was Ethiopic (T 202 675 2066), an Ethiopian restaurant still going strong next door to their more recent café. Bekele taught herself to bake and the couple put together a menu of small-batch breads, pâtisserie, pancakes and sandwiches, as well as more filling fare, including waffles, French toast and a 'breakfast pizza' (eggs, onions, cheddar, tomatoes and basil). The crisp, clean-lined interior has proved a hit with Batter Bowl's burgeoning clientele, which is mostly made up of neighbourhood folk. Sitting by the window with a paper and a coffee should set your day on its proper course. The café is open daily, 8am to 8pm, and also serves lunch.
403 H Street NE, T 202 675 2011, www.the-bbb.com

11.00 Connersmith

It's only in recent years that an exchange about the contemporary art world would include DC. This is due in part to Leigh Conner and Jamie Smith's gallery, which the duo launched in 1999, and the desire of the capital's young collectors to view art in their own city. Koen Vanmechelen ('Leaving Paradise', pictured) is among those US and foreign artists represented. *1358 Florida Avenue NE, T 202 588 8750*

14.00 National Portrait Gallery

There's a multitude of oils of men in wigs in this museum, thanks to the permanent collection covering America's origins. This includes Native Americans and European explorers through to Independence (one highlight being Gilbert Stuart's paintings of George Washington) and the Gilded Age. But even the early portraits are accessible and fascinating – they're on your level, not up on a horse. The contemporary sections span civil rights activists, showbiz, science and politics. One exhibition of paintings by Kehinde Wiley featured hip hop stars; think LL Cool J in the style of John Singer Sargent. In the middle of the building is an elegant courtyard (above), with a roof by Foster + Partners, which creates a serene space for the café and functions. *8th Street/F Street NW, T 202 633 8300, www.npg.si.edu*

20.00 Proof

Penn Quarter, or what was once referred to as Old Downtown, has been steadily rejuvenated to create a district offering dynamic cultural venues and top-notch dining. Tucked in next to the National Portrait Gallery (opposite), Proof is one of the most established restaurants in the area, boasting a contemporary interior by local architects GrizForm Design. There's a firm emphasis on wine (founder Mark Kuller is an ardent collector) and a strong selection of local and artisanal ingredients on chef Haidar Karoum's modern American menu; the cheeses and charcuterie are the high points. Vegetarian options do feature, but this is more a place for meat lovers. Try some wild boar salume from Utah, and crispy pig's head with parsley and lemon. *775 G Street NW, T 202 737 7663, www.proofdc.com*

22.30 Barmini
José Andrés is a tour de force on the DC dining scene, and this cocktail lounge adjacent to his acclaimed restaurant Minibar (T 202 393 0812) ups the ante. Before having a drink, consult with your mixologist, who will create something sublime. The interior, by architect Juli Capella and local firm CORE, is equally inspiring. Open Tuesday to Saturday.
855 E Street NW, T 202 393 4451

URBAN LIFE
CAFÉS, RESTAURANTS, BARS AND NIGHTCLUBS

DC's food scene isn't all carnivorous politicians in steakhouses and power breakfasts at the Four Seasons (see p029), although both are part of the mix. There are fabulous dining options courtesy of chefs with a national presence, such as José Andrés (see p038 and p046), and local talent like Cathal Armstrong at Restaurant Eve (110 S Pitt Street, Alexandria, T 703 706 0450), Chris Jakubiec at Plume (see p018) and Johnny Monis at Komi (1509 17th Street NW, T 202 332 9200) and Little Serow (1511 17th Street NW).

There is a healthy drinking culture too, as befits a town full of political obsessives, wealthy college kids and diplomats. Generally speaking, Georgetown attracts tourists, students and Southern Republicans in chinos and buttoned-down shirts, whereas Adams Morgan is ethnically and socially mixed, until the weekend, when suburbanites flood 18th Street. Then the hepcats of the inner city depart Adams Morgan and hit the bars and clubs of U Street/14th Street, the lounges and dives near Dupont Circle, and the chilled venues of newer hotspot H Street. Given that the Georgetown and George Washington universities are among the most expensive in America, they are a magnet for plutocratic students, Persian Gulf squillionaires, Brazilian property playboys and the like. Come the evening, many of them can be found sharing the exceptional view and a cocktail at the W's rooftop bar POV (see p054).

For full addresses, see Resources.

Dickson Wine Bar

The historic U Street district is a pleasant part of town to stroll around, and ideal for a casual glass of vino and a bite to eat. Many DC establishments that cater to a younger clientele have chosen to open up here, including the congenial Dickson Wine Bar. Tien Claudio and Steve Kaufmann took over the three-storey building with the pre-existing signage 'Dickson BLDG 903 You', hence the name, and tapped Jarad Slipp to put together a list of organic wines; organic ingredients appear in the cocktails too. Executive chef James Claudio devised a complementary environmentally friendly menu, which features hormone-free meats. Dickson's wood-lined interior is refreshingly unfussy, and includes a wall of backlit recycled wine bottles.
*903 U Street NW, T 202 332 1779,
www.dicksonwinebar.com*

Le Diplomate

Pierre Charles L'Enfant, the French architect who designed DC, drew partial inspiration from Paris. As did American restaurateur Stephen Starr for his local debut, this buzzy bistro, launched in 2013 north-west of Logan Circle. Taking over an old laundry building, Starr was faced with the challenge of transforming an industrial space into something more intimate. He turned to Shawn Hausman, a previous collaborator, who, along with Jessica Kimberley, shipped antiquities over from France and selected a rich red-and-gold colour palette, and hardwood and tiled flooring to achieve the Continental vibe. Adam Schop, whom Starr describes as 'an archaeologist of food', was installed as executive chef to deliver a cornucopia of French classics, from *fruits de mer* to *boudin blanc*. Reserve well in advance. *1601 14th Street NW, T 202 332 3333, www.lediplomatedc.com*

Astro

Doughnuts and fried chicken. The comfort food served at this Downtown joint is as American as it gets, but far from a gimmick. Washingtonians and former hockey players Elliot Spaisman and Jeff Halpern based the idea for the venture on their tradition of enjoying a doughnut together after a game. Jason Gehring, former pastry chef at the highly regarded DC restaurant Fiola and the modern brasserie Poste, joined the pair, bringing his grandmother's hallowed fried-chicken recipe out of his home and into the Astro kitchen. Doughnut flavours range from the classic and nostalgic – the Twinknut honours the Twinkie, which was recently threatened with extinction – to the exotic, like salted caramel with fleur de sel. Grandma would surely be proud. *1308 G Street NW, T 202 809 5565, www.astrodoughnuts.com*

Hank's Oyster Bar

Chef Jamie Leeds opened her first branch of Hank's (T 202 462 4265) in Dupont Circle in 2005, and has built a loyal fan base for her coastal cuisine. She named the venture after her fisherman father, Hank, and has even raised her own oyster, Hayden's Reef, in collaboration with Dragon Creek Aqua Farm, a business that uses oyster growing as a water-filtration method to improve the environment of Chesapeake Bay (see p096). Leeds' newer venue here in Capitol Hill is proving just as popular. There's an ice bar (with 50 per cent off after 10pm), offering raw oysters, tartare and ceviche, and the kitchen serves up New England classics like lobster rolls and Ipswich clams. If it's on the menu, try the Chesapeake Bay rockfish, the state fish of Maryland.
633 Pennsylvania Avenue SE,
T 202 733 1971, www.hanksoysterbar.com

Zaytinya

Under José Andrés, the mezze of Greece, Lebanon and Turkey became a hot eating trend in DC when the chef launched the Downtown Zaytinya in 2003. The food is still spot on, and the setting, by Adamstein & Demetriou, is a dramatic take on Greek island architecture. You enter into a large, two-storey, glass-fronted space, around which are smaller dining rooms looking on to the open kitchen and the adjoining outdoor terrace. A shelved marble wall separates the bar from the restaurant. The rest of the interior is all whitewashed surfaces, dark walnut, white marble and blackened steel. Order the Lebanese-style *kibbeh nayeh*, a beef tartare with bulgar wheat, radish and mint, and a *fattoush* salad, and imagine yourself by the Med.
701 9th Street NW, T 202 638 0800, www.zaytinya.com

Jack Rose Dining Saloon

A former boxing gym is arguably the ideal setting for a serious whisky bar. This was the thinking of the co-owners of Jack Rose, Washingtonians Bill Thomas and Stephen King. Incorporating several bars, as well as a restaurant and a terrace (above) with a retractable roof, the three-storey venue, converted by local architects Gronning, sits at the south end of Adams Morgans. Thomas deals with distributors across the country to ensure an ever-expanding selection of whiskies; the range currently includes a variety of vintages, proofs and finishes from sources such as India, Scotland, Kentucky and Washington State. In addition to scotch lovers, Jack Rose welcomes cigar aficionados, who can enjoy a leisurely smoke on the balcony. *2007 18th Street NW, T 202 588 7388, www.jackrosediningsaloon.com*

Birch & Barley
A good brunch has not always been
the easiest meal to find in DC, but this
Logan Circle restaurant has helped
to plug the gap. Artisanal beers are a
highlight, with more than 500 sourced
by Greg Engert. Kyle Bailey delivers
plenty of appetising dishes, and Tiffany
MacIsaac some knockout desserts. The
interior is by Catherine Hailey Design.
1337 14th Street NW, T 202 567 2576

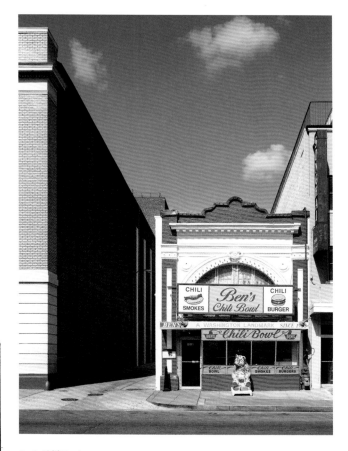

Ben's Chili Bowl

Ben's has been a U Street institution since 1958 – an African-American success story that has served chilli, cheese fries and hot dogs to everybody from Nat King Cole to Miles Davis. It survived the 1968 riots that destroyed U Street, and the heroin-dealing epidemic that devastated the community in the 1980s and 1990s. The building dates to 1910, when it housed a cinema showing silent films. It was later turned into a pool hall by Harry Beckley, one of DC's first black detectives. Today, it thrives under founder Ben Ali's sons, Kamal and Nizam, and their families, thanks partly to the revival of U Street. The signature dish is Bill Cosby's Original Chili Half-Smoke: a quarter-pound pork-and-beef hot dog with onions, chilli sauce and mustard. Have mints for afters. *1213 U Street NW, T 202 667 0909, www.benschilibowl.com*

Granville Moore's

Several decades ago, DC was almost as segregated as Johannesburg, with all the white people crammed into the affluent north-western quadrant. Rising property prices and improved racial attitudes then pushed gentrification east, first to U Street and now the burgeoning H Street corridor above Union Station, the location of this venue, a hip gastropub serving mussels and Belgian beers. The decor is scarred floorboards and antiqued wood, with salvaged fixtures. Granville Moore was an African-American doctor who lived in the building and treated the local poor for free. The pub's proprietor is Joe Englert, who also owns nearby music venue Rock & Roll Hotel (T 202 388 7625) and The Argonaut tavern (T 202 397 1416). *1238 H Street NE, T 202 399 2546, www.granvillemoores.com*

CityZen

Chef Eric Ziebold's résumé includes stints at DC's Vidalia and the acclaimed French Laundry in California. He then went on to produce his own modern American fare at CityZen, located in the Mandarin Oriental hotel. It wasn't long before the restaurant became a favourite of the city's foodies, a status it has maintained since its 2004 launch. The four-course prix fixe and the six-course tasting menus change daily, and may include delicacies such as foie gras risotto with roasted Granny Smith apples. Interior designer Tony Chi gave the chefs a copper-coloured performance space in the kitchen and used lighting that affords diners an intimate environment despite the lofty ceilings. Book well ahead or keep your fingers crossed for a cancellation. *1330 Maryland Avenue, T 202 787 6148, www.mandarinoriental.com/washington*

The Source by Wolfgang Puck

The first DC endeavour of Austrian chef and entrepreneur Wolfgang Puck is part of the Newseum, an interactive museum dedicated to news – hence the name. Housed in a glittery modern building just across from the National Gallery of Art (see p070), the multi-level restaurant has floor-to-ceiling windows and a two-storey, 2,000-bottle wine wall. It was given a clean, contemporary look by the Engstrom Design Group, with glass and wood predominating. The ground-floor bar/lounge is the more relaxed and casual setting, and the place for a quick bite from the modern Asian-inspired menu. Upstairs focuses on fine dining; order delicacies such as crispy suckling pig and lacquered Chinese duckling.

575 Pennsylvania Avenue NW, T 202 637 6100, www.wolfgangpuck.com

POV Roof Terrace
The bar topping the W hotel may well boast the best view in the city. Eleven floors above Pennsylvania Avenue, the monuments of the National Mall are laid out below, a vista that instils genuine awe. The crowd is eclectic, from military types to tourists, doctors and politicos. Don't swing by on a whim, as you must have a reservation, which can be booked online.
515 15th Street NW, www.pointofviewdc.com

Café Saint-Ex

This hangout is an anchor tenant for the revived U Street/14th Street 'hood. Named after Antoine de Saint-Exupéry, the French fighter pilot and author of *The Little Prince*, the ground-floor bar/restaurant is done out in dark colours and decorated with an aviation theme – there are propellers on the light shades. It's a little hokey, but the range of obscure beers and beautiful people in attendance make up for it. The menu focuses on American classics and seasonal ingredients. Downstairs is a lounge, Gate 54, where DJs play every night. The music ranges from jazz, bossa nova, soul and funk to electronica, Britpop and French mod-lounge. Saint-Ex is a happening weekend haunt for urbanites dodging the Adams Morgan crowds.
1847 14th Street NW, T 202 265 7839, www.saint-ex.com

Nopa Kitchen + Bar

This Penn Quarter brasserie was opened in 2013 by Ashok Bajaj, whose DC Indian restaurant Rasika (T 202 637 1222) has garnered national recognition since its launch in 2005. Nopa, which stands for north of Pennsylvania Avenue, is overseen by executive chef Greg McCarty, who has already excited foodies, thanks to dishes like his hot bread rolls layered with butter and herbs, and fried chicken. The menu mostly consists of American fare with occasional European and Asian influences in evidence. Martin Vahtra of the New York-based Projects Design Associates handled the design, giving the interiors a semi-industrial feel. There are distinct areas, including three private dining salons and a bar (above).
800 F Street NW, T 202 347 4667, www.nopadc.com

Charlie Palmer Steak

The steakhouse was once the archetypal Washington power restaurant – a place for the men (and they were always men) who ran America. Charlie Palmer, which has great views of the Capitol (see p009), is all that and more. Palmer made his name with his modern American cooking at Aureole in New York in the 1990s, and he currently has several highly regarded restaurants across the country. In DC, he brought in Martin Vahtra (see p057) to create a contemporary interior instead of the usual hunting prints and wood panelling. Much of the menu is presented in terms of numbers: 21- versus 28-day dry-aged Angus competes with Kobe strip loin, which is charged by the ounce. Fish, chicken and game dishes are also served. *101 Constitution Avenue NW, T 202 547 8100, www.charliepalmer.com*

Mintwood Place

Adams Morgan has long been a destination district in DC, due to its nightlife and dining scene. Mintwood Place has helped boost its appeal. Saied Azali, who also owns Perry's upstairs, launched the restaurant as a reasonably priced, reasonably casual spot to enjoy top-flight food. The interior was a collaboration between the architect Dave Rosenberg, Azali and John Cidre, and the bentwood chairs and antique tin walls give an impression of easy chic. French chef Cedric Maupillier applies his native culinary sensibility to the modern American menu, and cooks with a wood-burning oven in the kitchen. The outdoor patio is ideal for summer dining; in winter, snag a booth. The one drawback is the volume of noise, which can be loud.
1813 Columbia Road NW, T 202 234 6732, www.mintwoodplace.com

Maté
This Georgetown cocktail lounge, with a Latin-tinged sushi menu, has a grown-up feel and a sophisticated design. The interior, by local firm Grupo7, is post-industrial, with red walls, midcentury Panton 'Spiral' lamps, red 'Luna' chairs and an aluminium bar. Maté takes its name from the South American drink.
3101 K Street NW, T 202 333 2006, www.matedc.com

INSIDER'S GUIDE

CARLA CABRERA, BLOGGER

Bolivian-born Carla Cabrera, a full-time cancer research scientist who finds the time to write a fashion, food and culture blog, The President Wears Prada, moved to the DC area when she was 12 years old. She now lives near the National Portrait Gallery (see p036), one of the buildings that beguiled her when she arrived.

A typical day may entail an espresso at gelateria Dolcezza (1560 Wisconsin Avenue NW, T 202 333 4646), and lunch from one of DC's food trucks – she recommends Takorean (www.takorean.com), Red Hook Lobster Pound (www.redhooklobsterdc.com) and Pepe, whose chef is José Andrés (see p046). In the evening, she likes Dickson Wine Bar (see p041): 'It's intimate, has organic cocktails and the best *bánh mì* in town.' Cabrera is also a fan of the 10-seat Columbia Room within The Passenger (1021 7th Street NW, T 202 393 0220), overseen by master mixologist Derek Brown. Table (903 N Street NW, T 202 588 5200), which has a rooftop terrace, or Le Diplomate (see p042) are two of her dinner tips. Later, she'll head to the 9:30 Club (815 V Street NW, T 202 265 0930) to see live bands.

The Logan Circle neighbourhood is a favourite shopping haunt. She particularly likes GoodWood (1428 U Street NW, T 202 986 3640), which is full of 'curiosities'. When she has time off, Cabrera heads to the 1936 Meridian Hill Park (2400 15th Street NW), an urban oasis dotted with striking architecture.

For full addresses, see Resources.

ARCHITOUR
A GUIDE TO WASHINGTON'S ICONIC BUILDINGS

For an antebellum Southern city and imperial capital with classical pretensions, there's a surprising amount of DC architecture that does not involve columns. Of course, the federal funding of much of the city helps; enlightened bureaucrats in the late postwar era commissioned the world's finest architects to produce museums, memorials and government offices. That's how IM Pei, Gordon Bunshaft and Marcel Breuer left their mark on Washington.

The capital's function as a place where foreign representatives are based has also paid dividends. Embassies, especially in a rich economy, can be a shop window for your best design brains. The Scandinavians have certainly pursued this policy, with Vilhelm Lauritzen's glass-and-steel Danish Embassy (3200 Whitehaven Street NW, T 202 234 4300), finished in 1960, being a fine example.

We have concentrated on central public buildings – except the Dulles Airport Terminal (see p078), as presumably you will land there – but if you have the means to get about, there are many domestic gems to see. Frank Lloyd Wright's Pope-Leighey House (9000 Richmond Highway, Alexandria, T 703 780 4000) is open to visitors. Closer in, the Forest Hills district, between Rock Creek Park and Connecticut Avenue, is the location of several midcentury modern homes, including the only one in DC designed by Richard Neutra, the 1968 Brown House (3005 Audubon Terrace NW). *For full addresses, see Resources.*

Hirshhorn Museum

The late American architecture critic Ada Louise Huxtable dubbed Gordon Bunshaft's circular concrete building 'neo-penitentiary modern', and many others have reverted to the 'bunker' clichés. Yet SOM's avowed minimalist was only following orders. The Smithsonian requested a contemporary art gallery that would be unlike the rest of the museums on the National Mall. Pritzker winner Bunshaft duly gave them a cylinder elevated on four 'legs', with a fountain occupying the central courtyard and windows lining the inner wall. The form facilitates a flow of space around and under the structure, while expressing the internal layout of the gallery space. The architect's original sculpture garden was remodelled by Lester Collins in 1981. *Independence Avenue SW/7th Street, T 202 633 1000, www.hirshhorn.si.edu*

House of Sweden
Unlike most embassies, Gert Wingårdh
and Tomas Hansen's exceptional design
presents an open face to the world. Light
is a key element – the 2006 blondwood,
stone and glass structure is suffused
with it. After dark, illumination gives
the sense that the building is floating
above its reflection in the Potomac.
2900 K Street NW, T 202 536 1500,
www.houseofsweden.com

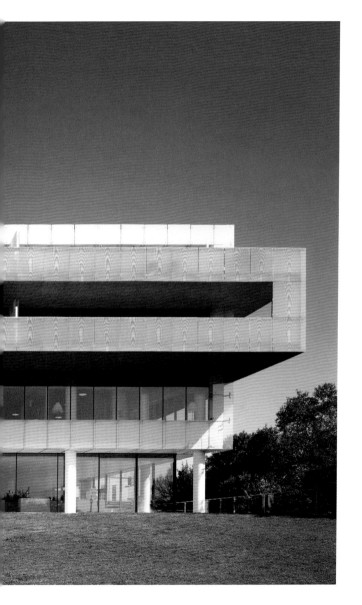

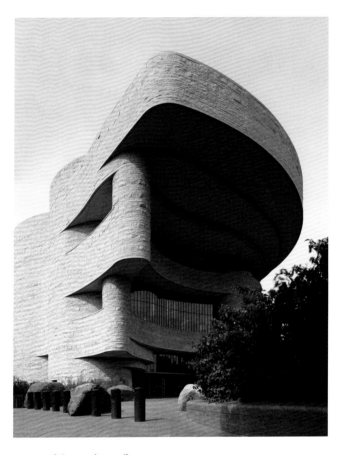

Museum of the American Indian

Native Americans have often suffered in museums, turning up in tacky dioramas near the dinosaurs. This one collaborates with indigenous populations throughout the western hemisphere to ensure the native peoples it features have a say in the context in which they are placed. A key part of that consultation is the structure itself – a dramatic curvilinear building constructed from Kasota limestone with a cliff-like entrance that's reminiscent of a desert outcrop. Completed in 2004, the museum was designed by Canadian architect Douglas Cardinal but with input from Native American community leaders. The many stories of genocide, betrayal and marginalisation told within it are sure to provoke both anger and sadness.
*4th Street/Independence Avenue SW,
T 202 633 1000, www.nmai.si.edu*

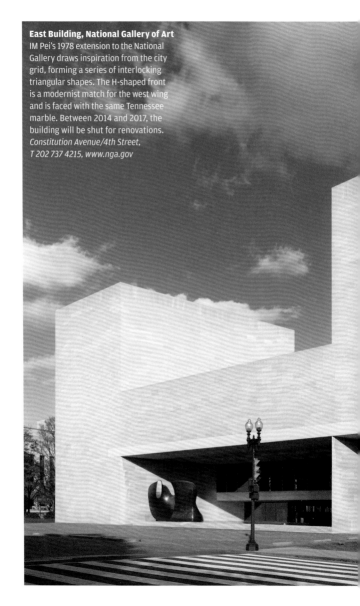

East Building, National Gallery of Art
IM Pei's 1978 extension to the National
Gallery draws inspiration from the city
grid, forming a series of interlocking
triangular shapes. The H-shaped front
is a modernist match for the west wing
and is faced with the same Tennessee
marble. Between 2014 and 2017, the
building will be shut for renovations.
*Constitution Avenue/4th Street,
T 202 737 4215, www.nga.gov*

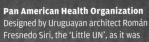

Pan American Health Organization
Designed by Uruguayan architect Román
Fresnedo Siri, the 'Little UN', as it was
called when it was inaugurated in 1965,
reveals a Corbusian influence in the piers
that hold up the main secretariat building.
The latticed cylindrical mass in front
functions as a 275-seat council chamber.
Tours are organised through the DC
Preservation League (T 202 783 5144).
525 23rd Street NW, T 202 974 3000

Martin Luther King Jr Memorial Library

One of Mies van der Rohe's last buildings (it was dedicated after he died in 1972), this library is his only structure in DC. Poor maintenance and cost-cutting during construction meant it was plagued with malfunctioning elevators, temperature control problems and leaks. However, it was designated a National Landmark in 2007. Repairs were initiated and the Mies-designed 'Brno' and 'Barcelona' chairs that had been in the library at the time of its launch were tracked down and reinstalled. Interior renovations have been carried out by the DC-based Bell Architects. The building remains a crisply beautiful slice of late modernism, its black-steel-grid facade replicated by the shelving inside, which is visible when lit up at night.
901 G Street NW, T 202 727 0321, www.dclibrary.org

New Residence at the Swiss Embassy
Another nominee for best in embassy row has to be the Swiss ambassador's residence in Woodley Park. The 2006 design was a joint effort between Swiss practice Rüssli and Steven Holl Architects. The two firms conceived a structure that, according to the embassy, was inspired by 'the rugged snow-covered Alps of Switzerland'. Its cruciform shape has front elevations built using charcoal-coloured concrete trimmed in local slate, while other facades comprise sandblasted glass planks. The remaining walls are made of glass panels that function as transparent and semi-transparent dividers between the inside and outside. The building is also highly energy efficient. Its flat roof is sown with sedum and the south-facing walls use passive solar energy.
2900 Cathedral Avenue, T 202 745 7900, www.swissemb.org

HUD Headquarters
Marcel Breuer's massive expressionist
HQ for the Department of Housing and
Urban Development (HUD), completed
in 1968, dominates its site, perched
on dainty paired piloti that taper to the
ground. Above, the curved concrete
structure forms the shape of a truncated,
stubby X. The underused plaza was re-
landscaped by Martha Schwartz in 1998.
451 7th Street SW. T 202 708 1112

Dulles Airport Terminal

Named after the high priest of American imperialism, John Foster Dulles, and opened in 1962, at the height of the Cold War, Eero Saarinen's swooping masterpiece was the first American airport designed expressly for the jet age. The massive roof is reinforced with steel and supported by columns that are 15.2m high on the airfield side and 20.7m high on the approach side, which gives the structure its distinctive hanging-curve shape. In-between the columns there are glass curtain walls. The slope of the piers was exaggerated by Saarinen beyond their structural need, in order to increase the dynamic effect of the form. The terminal was also designed so that it could be seamlessly expanded at either end, which happened in 1996.
Chantilly, Virginia, T 703 572 2700, www.mwaa.com/dulles

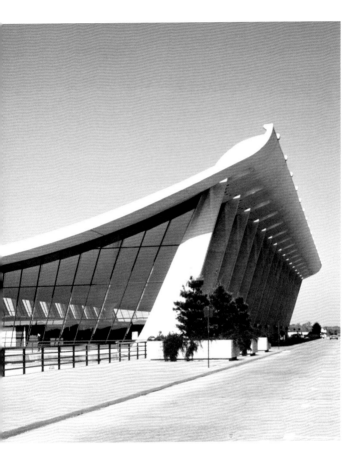

SHOPPING

THE BEST RETAIL THERAPY AND WHAT TO BUY

The historical truth about DC retail is that many of the locals who wanted to make it in fashion or design soon hoofed it up to New York, but this has been changing in recent years. Washingtonians have become more discerning in their tastes and demands, and there is a greater call for a local spin on products. Redeem (1810 14th Street NW, T 202 332 7447) is a good example. Launched in 2006 by Lori Parkerson, a native and former radio DJ, the shop carries an array of homegrown designers, in addition to hard-to-find American labels, and has a lively events scene linked to the boutique. Over in Georgetown, Major (1426 Wisconsin Avenue NW, T 202 625 6732) is owned and operated by California transplant Duk-ki Yu, an avid sneaker collector who detected a gap in the DC market for an edgier selection of treads.

Mainstream and upmarket brands line Wisconsin Avenue and M Street in Georgetown. There are a few surviving independent stores here, like Hu's Shoes (3005 M Street NW, T 202 342 0202), which is one of the best places in town for footwear by the likes of Alexander Wang or Chie Mihara. The area to scour for interiors is the U Street/14th Street corridor; Millennium Decorative Arts (1528 U Street NW, T 202 483 1218) is worth checking out for its range of second-hand modernist pieces. While you're in the area, call into Federal (see p085), which sells men's fashion.

For full addresses, see Resources.

Atelier Takagi

Working out of a studio to the north of Georgetown, Jonah Takagi is one of DC's foremost industrial designers, and has collaborated with Wallpaper* on several occasions. The son of an architect, he was drawn to the question of how things are put together from an early age, pursuing his curiosity through a degree at Rhode Island School of Design and his own atelier, which he set up in 2009. Surface finish and natural materials are key to his work, which ranges from homewares to lighting and furniture. The 'Bluff City' pendant (above), created for Roll & Hill in 2011, was inspired by the trouble lights of the 20th century; it's on sale at Design Within Reach (T 202 339 9480). In 2012, Takagi co-founded the online design store Field. *3857 Beecher Street NW, T 1 503 957 9911, www.ateliertakagi.com*

Daniel Donnelly Modern Design Studio

When Daniel Donnelly set up shop in 1986, local furniture tastes were all for the chintzy, the overstuffed, the loose-covered and the oversized. Put off by all this, and the 'ugly brown' antiques that his parents had sold, he got himself in at the beginning of the midcentury modern design revival. He has survived for more than 25 years by luring DC's interiors hipsters out to his Alexandria warehouse/store, where the range of vintage items, sold in varying conditions, is probably the best in the region. In addition, Donnelly stocks reissues of classics by Modernica, Herman Miller, Knoll, Isokon Plus and ICF, as well as textiles and a selection of his own cabinetry designs, which echo the furniture of the 1940s, 1950s and 1960s. A custom upholstery service is also offered. Closed Tuesdays and Wednesdays.
520 N Fayette Street, Alexandria,
T 703 549 4672, www.danieldonnelly.com

Kramerbooks

A Dupont Circle institution since it opened in 1976, Kramerbooks is a big first-date destination for DC's literati – if it's going well, you can move to the coffee shop at the back, Afterwords Café, which also has a terrace area at the front. The bookstore has two entrances and is crammed full of an eclectic assortment of titles, with particularly strong sections on politics (natch), contemporary literature and travel. The Dupont district is populated by embassies, students and a large gay community, so Kramerbooks' selection unsurprisingly veers towards the liberal and internationalist. Do like a local and stay a while, browse, or get a bite to eat. Open daily, from 7.30am to 1am, and 24 hours on Fridays and Saturdays.
1517 Connecticut Avenue NW,
T 202 387 1400, www.kramers.com

Federal

Situated off Florida Avenue, Federal sells a selection of hip menswear, including lines not readily available elsewhere in the city. Greg Grammen, originally from Alexandria, opened the store next door to his skate shop and urban nerve centre Palace 5ive (T 202 299 9008), which he named after the DC-based basketball team of the 1920s. Paying allegiance to retro American workwear, Federal stocks an abundance of raw denim, along with Red Wing boots, the requisite Pendleton blankets and a range of accessories. To drive the manly theme home, the interior is dotted with vintage *Playboy* magazines and books on muscle cars. Further along 14th Street, check out Redeem (see p080), another good source of domestic fashion.
2216 14th Street NW, T 202 518 3375, www.federalstoredc.com

G Fine Art
Occupying the second floor of an
industrial building, G Fine Art focuses
on works from the 1960s onwards. Art
advisor and the gallery's owner Annie
Gawlak, who is married to the painter
Sam Gilliam, founded the space in 2001.
Previous exhibitors have included Dan
Steinhilber (*Untitled*, pictured), who
lives and works in Washington DC.
1350 Florida Avenue NE, T 202 462 1601

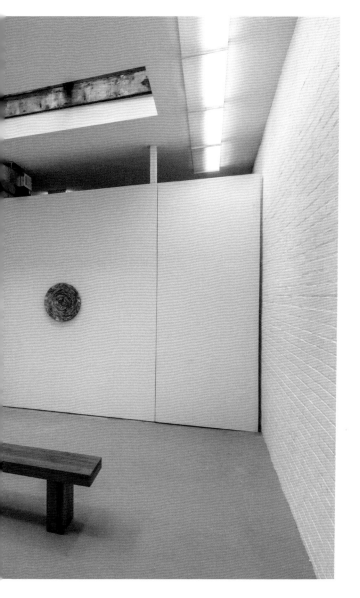

SPORTS AND SPAS

WORK OUT, CHILL OUT OR JUST WATCH

Spectator sports in Washington mean a choice between watching the giant suburban titan that is the Redskins, one of the NFL's most successful teams, and the rather more modest Nationals baseball team, who not long ago were the equally modest Montreal Expos. Redskins tickets are like gold dust, despite FedExField (1600 Fedex Way, T 301 276 6000) in Maryland having 79,000 seats; your best bet is to stump up online. The Nationals, however, are so keen to bring in fans that they have been known to run free transport; it's probably more convenient to catch a regular bus from outside the bars on Pennsylvania Avenue behind the Capitol (see p009). Only an actual baseball fan can judge if the quality is good or bad. For the rest of us, the distinction, in this stop-start sport, is slim.

If it's pampering you're after, you are in luck. Spas are one of the ways in which DC's high-end hotels have chosen to compete. The one at the Four Seasons (see p029) is delightful (non-guests must book a treatment), as are those at many of the top hotels; we recommend the Mandarin Oriental (see p092). If you want to exercise DC-style, hit the Mall, where the real West Wingers (and others) put in the miles every morning before going into the office to run the world. Ice-skaters have two options, the rink at The Yards Park (see p090), or the Pentagon Row Ice Skating rink (1201 South Joyce Street, T 703 418 6666) across the river in Arlington. *For full addresses, see Resources.*

Mint

This is the kind of gym that gets criticised by muscle-heads for being insufficiently hard core, which makes it our kind of gym. Mint is quiet, clean and soothing, and also boasts a good juice bar, Purée, floor-to-ceiling windows and free wi-fi. Member numbers are capped to stop it getting too busy, but an out-of-town visitor is able to purchase passes for $30 (one day) or $75 (three days). Owners Patrick and Melissa John were keen to open a place that was more than just a workout zone, and they describe Mint as an 'urban retreat'. In addition to the gym facilities, it offers all the usual studio classes, including cardio, spinning, core, yoga and Pilates, and the spa treatments include facials, waxing, spray tanning and a variety of massages. *1724 California Street NW, T 202 328 6468, www.mintdc.com*

The Yards Park

A decade ago, the neighbourhood by the Anacostia River near the US Navy Yard was a place to avoid. It was neither safe nor desirable. Today, locals flock to the newly created Yards Park, a public space that's transformed the Capitol Riverfront district and provided a mini-getaway for overwrought city dwellers. The New York firm M Paul Friedberg and Partners, who specialise in urban design, embraced the area's heritage, installing fountains, a shallow pool with a waterfall, lawns, a boardwalk, and wave-like benches, all anchored by a spiralling pedestrian bridge that is as much sculpture as it is utility. The sporting facilities include strolling or jogging paths next to the water and an ice rink in winter. There's also a theatre stage for concerts.
3rd/4th Streets SE, www.yardspark.org

Spa at Mandarin Oriental

They have thought of everything at this temple to the senses, where treatments that combine light and water, and colour and scent, are prevalent. There are two beauty suites, an aromatherapy Crystal Steam Room, a colour therapy Experience Shower, an Ice Fountain and a swimming pool (opposite), among other facilities. In one of the eight sleek rooms, you can receive an expertly administered oriental bamboo massage, deep-tissue pummelling or a less taxing cherry-blossom scrub – an invigorating all-over body ritual that uses warm exfoliating cream, rice powder and aromatic shea butter. It is, of course, all wonderfully relaxing. We especially like the Tibetan finger cymbals that begin and conclude each of the treatments.
1330 Maryland Avenue, T 202 787 6100, www.mandarinoriental.com/washington

Rock Creek Park Tennis Center
In 1969, Arthur Ashe had the idea of
holding a tennis tournament in a racially
integrated part of DC to open the game
up to all. It was a temporary set-up
until a 7,500-seater stadium, 25 outdoor
courts and five indoor were put up in
1989. The venue hosts the annual Citi
Open tournament, prior to the US Open.
16th Street/Kennedy Street, T 202 722
5949, www.rockcreektennis.com

ESCAPES

WHERE TO GO IF YOU WANT TO LEAVE TOWN

Washington's hinterland is America's old country. Whether it's in the moneyed hills of Virginia surrounding Middleburg, or the sun-bleached, crab-filled Chesapeake Bay, accommodation usually has 'inn' as part of the name and is more historic brick than glass-and-wood contemporary. That's not to say there aren't edgier places to explore. Baltimore (see p100) comes with a dicey but improving reputation, whereas Richmond, Virginia, has a cool music scene and a Museum of Fine Arts (opposite). Annapolis in Maryland is a good stepping-off point for the Chesapeake shores, and, together with resort towns like St Michaels, offers opportunities for messing about in boats and eating the catch of the day. What they forgo in aesthetics, Maryland's seafood shacks make up for with freshness. Try Stoney's Seafood House (3939 Oyster House Road, Broomes Island, T 410 586 1888), which has a deck on the water.

For architectural stimulation, take a trip to Frank Lloyd Wright's Fallingwater (see p102) in Pennsylvania, a sublime building at one with its environment. Or you could travel to Annapolis to view Richard Neutra's 1959 Mellon Hall at St John's College, one of the architect's most important buildings on the East Coast. The town also has more Georgian streets than anywhere else in America. Pushing into West Virginia, seclude yourself away at Lost River Modern (see p098), a contemporary cabin in an Arcadian setting. *For full addresses, see Resources.*

Virginia Museum of Fine Arts

Founded and built during the Depression, as a testament to the importance and the rejuvenating powers of art, the 1936 VMFA has been expanding its buildings, grounds and collections ever since. On display is an impressive variety of works, from American painting to art deco furnishings. In 2010, the museum unveiled a major extension designed by London-based architect Rick Mather in collaboration with Richmond firm SMBW. Encompassing a brand-new wing (above), connected to two existing gallery areas via a large atrium, and an attractive sculpture garden, the project has garnered several architectural awards. Had there been any doubt, VMFA's status as one of the region's outstanding arts museums was confirmed.

200 N Boulevard, Richmond, Virginia, T 804 340 1400, www.vmfa.state.va.us

Lost River Modern, West Virginia

Chris Brown and his wife, Sarah Johnson, wanted a getaway from their busy DC lives. They decided the solution was to build a modern prefab in Lost River, two hours' drive from the city. Designed by New York firm Resolution: 4 Architecture, the cedar-clad cabin features a deck and two-level interior with a large expanse of glass to allow light to stream in. Added bonuses are the modernist furnishings and wood-fired Dutch tub. Set on a 12-hectare plot, this sleek bolthole shouldn't afford you too many reasons to leave, but if you do want to go exploring, hike over to Cranny Crow in nearby Lost River State Park, from where the views of the surrounding mountains are spectacular. Alternatively, relax, breathe, and don't think about anything much at all.
www.lostrivermodern.com

Baltimore

The 1878 George Peabody Library (above; T 410 234 4943), designed by Edmund G Lind, and Thomas Lamb's 1914 Hippodrome Theatre (opposite; T 410 837 7400), now called the France-Merrick Performing Arts Center, are evidence of the wealth that this city once generated as a seaport. But the working-class town was one of the first to go into recession in the 20th century. It was badly damaged in the 1968 riots and for much of the 1970s it was known for its high crime rate and urban decay, as well as the films of John Waters. In the 1980s, it became the blueprint for a hundred urban regeneration schemes, from Boston to Liverpool, when investment in its inner harbour created a pleasant zone of shops and eateries. Today, the city has a strong, witty sense of itself. One of the best places to stay is the Hilton (T 443 573 8700).

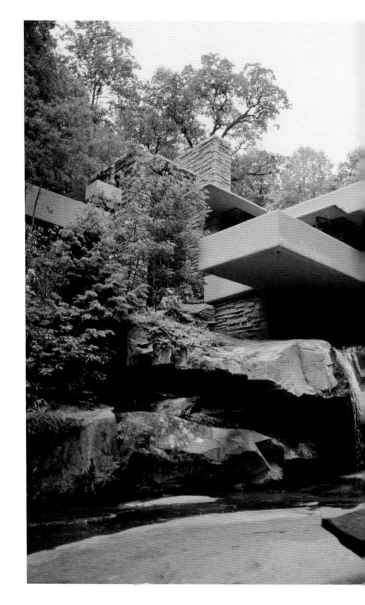

Fallingwater, Pennsylvania

Three-and-a-half hours' drive from DC is Fallingwater, voted the most important building in the States by the American Institute of Architects. Frank Lloyd Wright was in his sixties and looking past his best when he met the wealthy and urbane Kaufmanns of Pittsburgh, who wanted a weekend retreat built in south-western Pennsylvania. He designed a cantilevered masterpiece whose concrete terraces (left) echo the rocky ledges of the Bear Run waterfall. In location, layout and use of materials, Fallingwater is the synthesis of FLW's beliefs about organic architecture, and is so utterly in step with its setting that regular maintenance is required by the preservation group that manages it to tackle tree roots and all that rushing water.
1491 Mill Run Road, Mill Run,
T 724 329 8501, www.fallingwater.org

NOTES
SKETCHES AND MEMOS

RESOURCES

CITY GUIDE DIRECTORY

HOTELS

ADDRESSES AND ROOM RATES

Capella 020
Room rates:
double, from $495;
Georgetown Room, from $945;
Suite, from $1,445
1050 31st Street NW
T 202 617 2400
www.capellahotels.com/washingtondc

Donovan House 030
Room rates:
double, from $150;
Studio King Suite, from $250
1155 14th Street NW
T 202 737 1200
www.donovanhousehotel.com

Four Seasons 029
Room rates:
double, from $570;
Presidential Suite 478, from $11,400;
Royal Suite 278, price on request
2800 Pennsylvania Avenue NW
T 202 342 0444
www.fourseasons.com/washington

Hilton Baltimore 101
Room rates:
double, from $140
401 West Pratt Street
Baltimore
Maryland
T 443 573 8700
www.baltimore.hilton.com

The Jefferson 018
Room rates:
double, from $300;
Deluxe Room, from $400
1200 16th Street NW
T 202 448 2300
www.jeffersondc.com

Lost River Modern 098
Room rates:
Cabin, from $200
West Virginia
www.lostrivermodern.com

The Mayflower Renaissance 026
Room rates:
double, from $130;
Room 776, from $130
1127 Connecticut Avenue NW
T 202 347 3000
www.marriott.com

Hotel Monaco 024
Room rates:
double, from $215;
Monte Carlo Room 316, $290
700 F Street NW
T 202 628 7177
www.monaco-dc.com

Hotel Palomar 027
Room rates:
double, from $260;
Room 922, from $270;
Executive King, from $380;
Room 939, from $450
2121 P Street NW
T 202 448 1800
www.hotelpalomardc.com

Park Hyatt 028
Room rates:
double, from $250;
Room 916, from $325
1201 24th Street NW
T 202 789 1234
www.parkwashington.hyatt.com

WALLPAPER* CITY GUIDES

Executive Editor
Rachael Moloney

Authors
Alix Lambert
Paul McCann

Art Director
Loran Stosskopf
Art Editor
Eriko Shimazaki
Designer
Mayumi Hashimoto
Map Illustrator
Russell Bell

Photography Editor
Elisa Merlo
Assistant Photography Editor
Nabil Butt

Chief Sub-Editor
Nick Mee
Sub-Editor
Farah Shafiq

Editorial Assistant
Emma Harrison

Interns
Elisabetta D'Addario
Luba Kozorezova
Albert Sabás

Wallpaper* Group Editor-in-Chief
Tony Chambers
Publishing Director
Gord Ray
Managing Editor
Oliver Adamson

Wallpaper* ® is a
registered trademark
of IPC Media Limited

First published 2009
Revised and updated 2014

All prices are correct at
the time of going to press,
but are subject to change.

Printed in China

PHAIDON

Phaidon Press Limited
Regent's Wharf
All Saints Street
London N1 9PA

Phaidon Press Inc
180 Varick Street
New York, NY 10014

Phaidon® is a registered
trademark of Phaidon
Press Limited

www.phaidon.com

A CIP Catalogue record for
this book is available from
the British Library.

ISBN 978 0 7148 6649 9

PHOTOGRAPHERS

**Age Fotostock/
Superstock**
Fallingwater, pp102-103

**Cameron Davidson/
Alamy**
Washington DC city view,
inside front cover

Uyen Le/Alamy
Museum of the American
Indian, p068

Angelo Hornak/Corbis
Dulles Airport
Terminal, pp078-079

Loren Fiedler
The Jefferson, pp018-019
Capella, p020, p021
Batter Bowl Bakery, p033
Connersmith, pp034-035
Proof, p037
Barmini, pp038-039
Dickson Wine Bar, p041
Le Diplomate, pp042-043
Astro, p044
Hank's Oyster Bar, p045
Jack Rose Dining
Saloon, p047
Birch & Barley, pp048-049
POV Roof
Terrace, pp054-055
Nopa Kitchen + Bar, p057
Mintwood Place, p059

Carla Cabrera, p063
Federal, p085
G Fine Art, pp086-087
The Yards Park,
pp090-091

Travis Fullerton
Virginia Museum of Fine
Arts, p097

Timothy Hursley
National Portrait
Gallery, p036

Chris Mueller
Lost River Modern,
pp098-099

Michael David Rose
The Willard
InterContinental, p017
Hotel Tabard Inn,
p022, p023
Hotel Monaco, pp024-025
The Mayflower
Renaissance, p026
Hotel Palomar, p027
Park Hyatt, p028
Four Seasons, p029
Zaytinya, p046
Ben's Chili Bowl, p050
Granville Moore's, p051
CityZen, p052
The Source by Wolfgang
Puck, p053
Café Saint-Ex, p056
Charlie Palmer

Steak, p058
Maté, pp060-061
Hirshhorn Museum, p065
House of Sweden,
pp066-067
Museum of the American
Indian, p069
Martin Luther King Jr
Memorial Library, p074
Daniel Donnelly Modern
Design Studio, pp082-083
Kramerbooks, p084
Mint, p089
Rock Creek Park Tennis
Center, pp094-095

Andy Ryan
White House, pp010-011
Watergate Complex,
pp012-013
Lincoln Memorial,
pp014-015
East Building, National
Gallery of Art, pp070-071
Pan American Health
Organization, pp072-073
New Residence at the
Swiss Embassy, p075
HUD Headquarters,
pp076-077

Keith Weller
France-Merrick Performing
Arts Center, p100

WASHINGTON DC
A COLOUR-CODED GUIDE TO THE HOT 'HOODS

GEORGETOWN
This posh residential area is a popular weekend draw for its boutique and bar scene

ADAMS MORGAN
It pioneered racial integration in the 1950s, and now this lively area attracts all-comers

NATIONAL MALL
As seen on TV sets worldwide. Visit the seats of American power and myriad monuments

U STREET/14TH STREET CORRIDOR
The once derelict African-American district has reinvented itself as an arty, leftfield hub

FOGGY BOTTOM
Modernism does exist in DC after all, among the high-end hotels of this venerable district

DOWNTOWN
Business towers, galleries, Chinatown and architectural gems form an interesting mix

DUPONT CIRCLE
Originally anti-establishment but now more corporate, Dupont has a sophisticated vibe

CAPITOL HILL
Listen in on the latest gossip as you encounter government workers in their backyard

For a full description of each neighbourhood, see the Introduction.
Featured venues are colour-coded, according to the district in which they are located.